This Boxer Books paperback belongs to

. . . .

www.boxerbooks.com

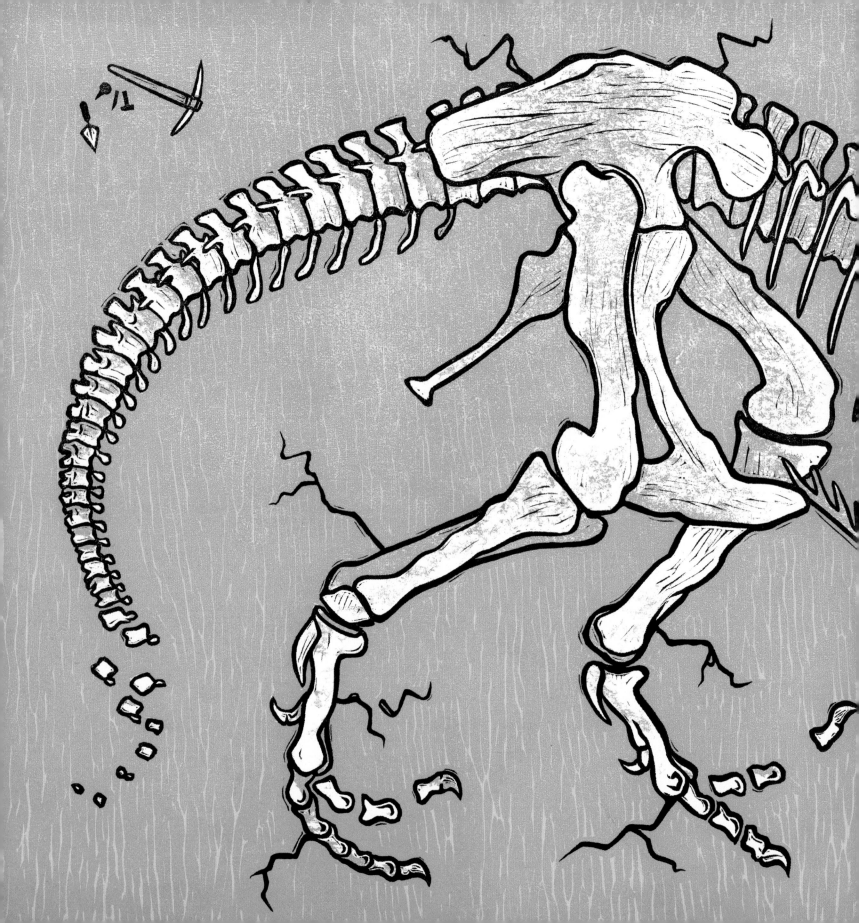

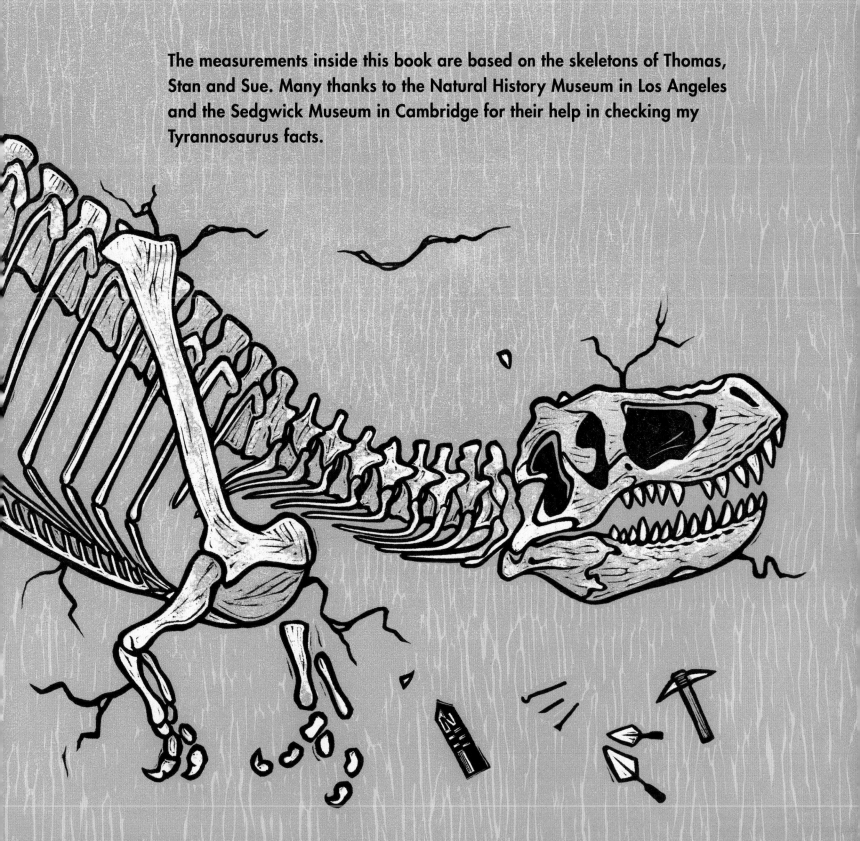

The measurements inside this book are based on the skeletons of Thomas, Stan and Sue. Many thanks to the Natural History Museum in Los Angeles and the Sedgwick Museum in Cambridge for their help in checking my Tyrannosaurus facts.

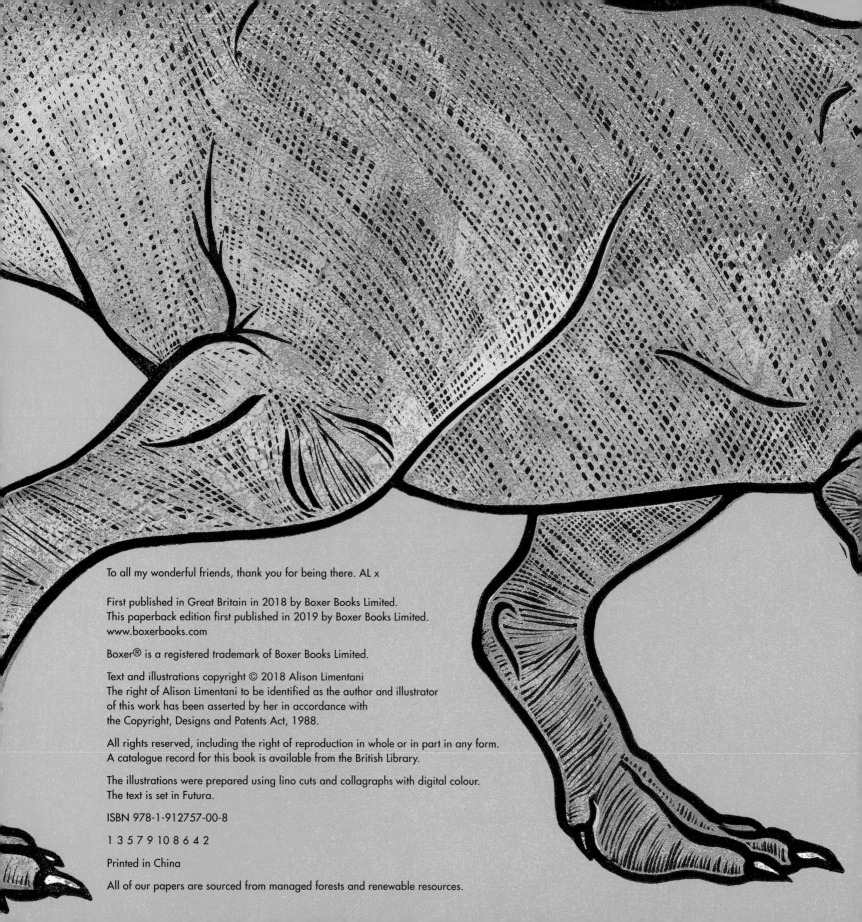

To all my wonderful friends, thank you for being there. AL x

First published in Great Britain in 2018 by Boxer Books Limited.
This paperback edition first published in 2019 by Boxer Books Limited.
www.boxerbooks.com

Boxer® is a registered trademark of Boxer Books Limited.

Text and illustrations copyright © 2018 Alison Limentani
The right of Alison Limentani to be identified as the author and illustrator
of this work has been asserted by her in accordance with
the Copyright, Designs and Patents Act, 1988.

The illustrations were prepared using lino cuts and collagraphs with digital colour.
The text is set in Futura.

ISBN 978-1-912757-00-8

1 3 5 7 9 10 8 6 4 2

Printed in China

All of our papers are sourced from managed forests and renewable resources.

HOW TALL
WAS A
T. REX?

ALISON LIMENTANI

BOXER BOOKS

A T. rex might have been scaly like a reptile,

or feathered like a bird.

Its eyes were as big as baseballs.

baseball   cricket   tennis   pool   golf

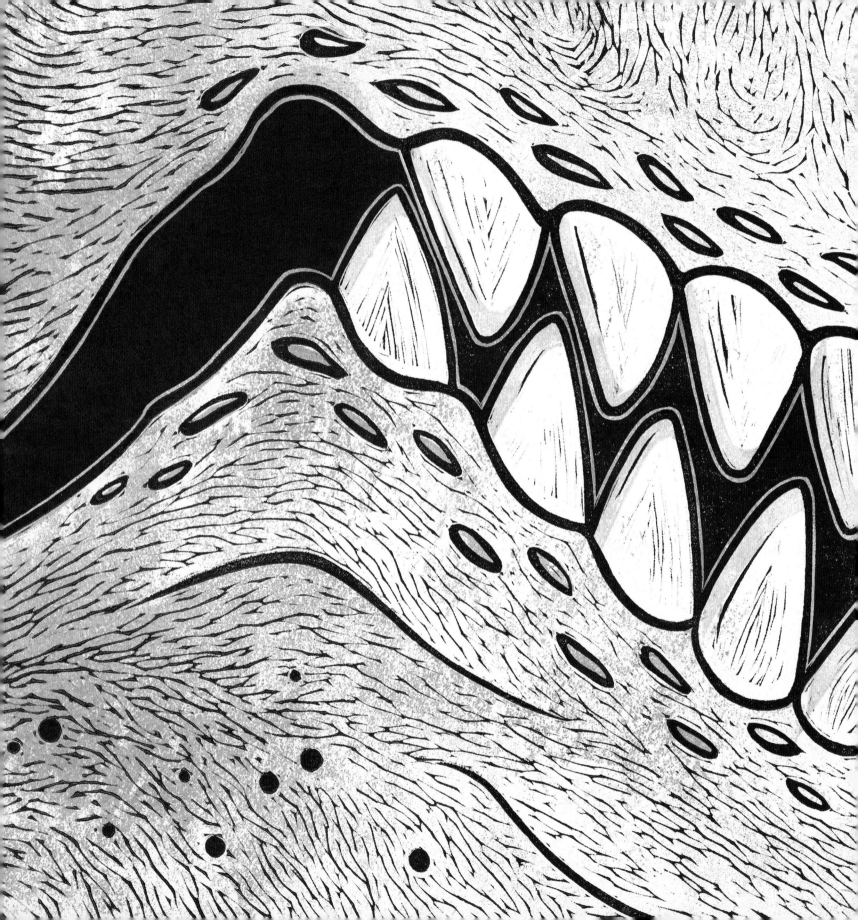

Its teeth were as big as bananas.

A T. rex could have eaten a goat in one gulp!

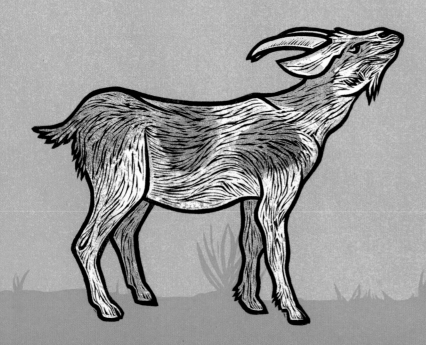

It was as heavy as 3 hippos.

2,500kg

2,500kg

2,500kg

7,500kg

And as long as 6 lions.

A T. rex could have run as fast as an elephant or a meerkat,

10–25
mph

70
mph

but slower than a cheetah.

37 children's footprints could fit inside one T. rex footprint!

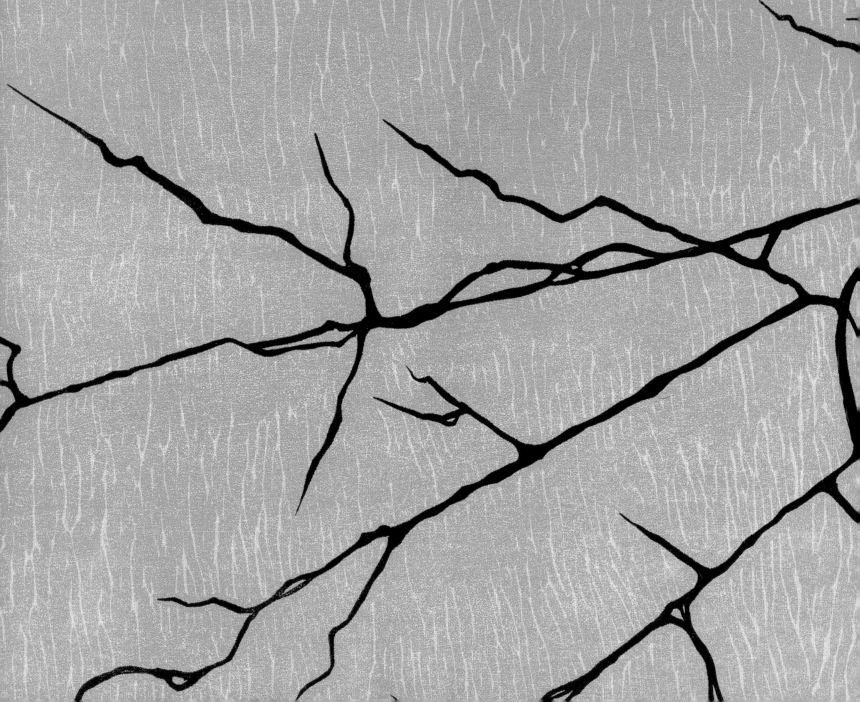

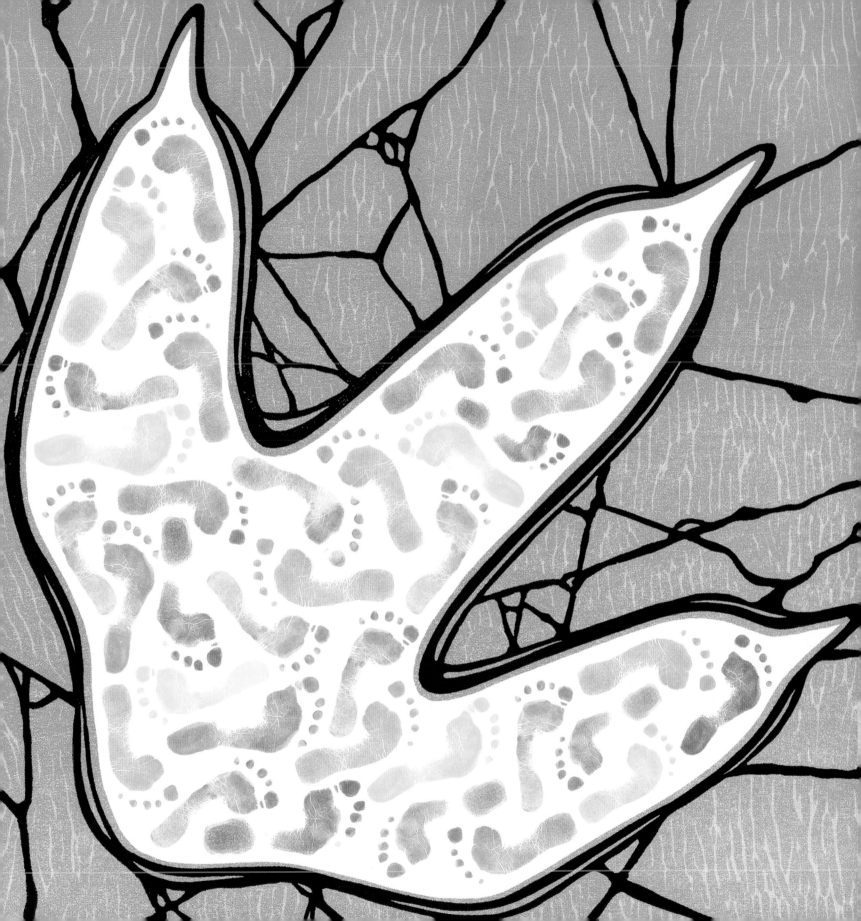

But how tall was a T. rex?

A T. rex was as tall as
10 velociraptors.

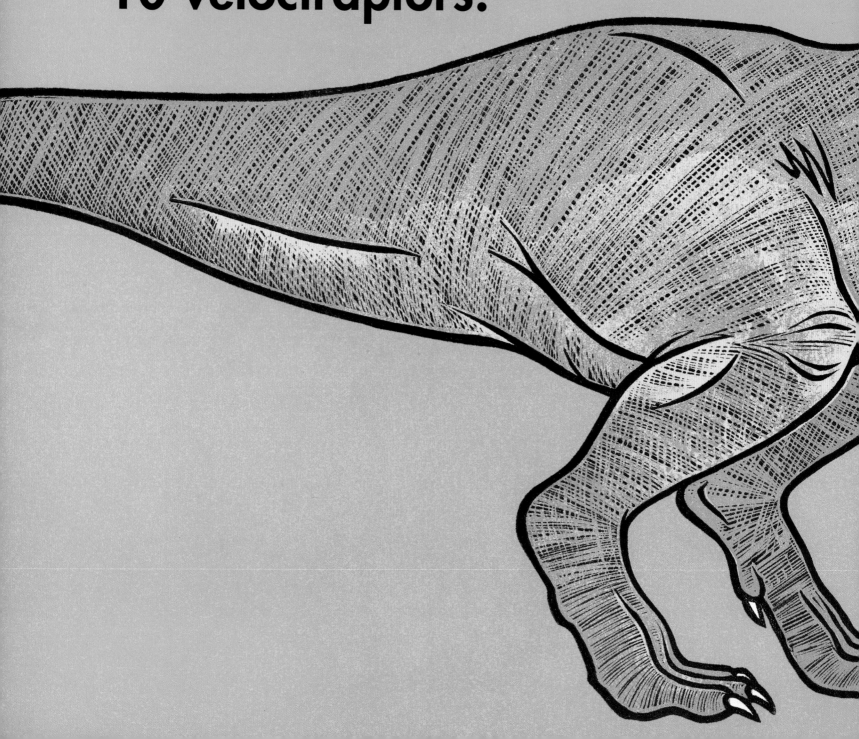

Or half as tall as a brachiosaurus.

Or as tall as a giraffe!

Scientists can tell a lot about dinosaurs by looking at bones and fossils. The facts in this book are based on what we currently think about the Tyrannosaurus rex, but who knows what we'll discover in the future!

Skull length = up to 1.45m

Eye sockets = up to 12cm

Tooth length = up to 25cm

Head to tail length = up to 12m

Height to hips = up to 4m
(Total reach estimated at 5m)

Height = 30–50cm

Height = 9–15m

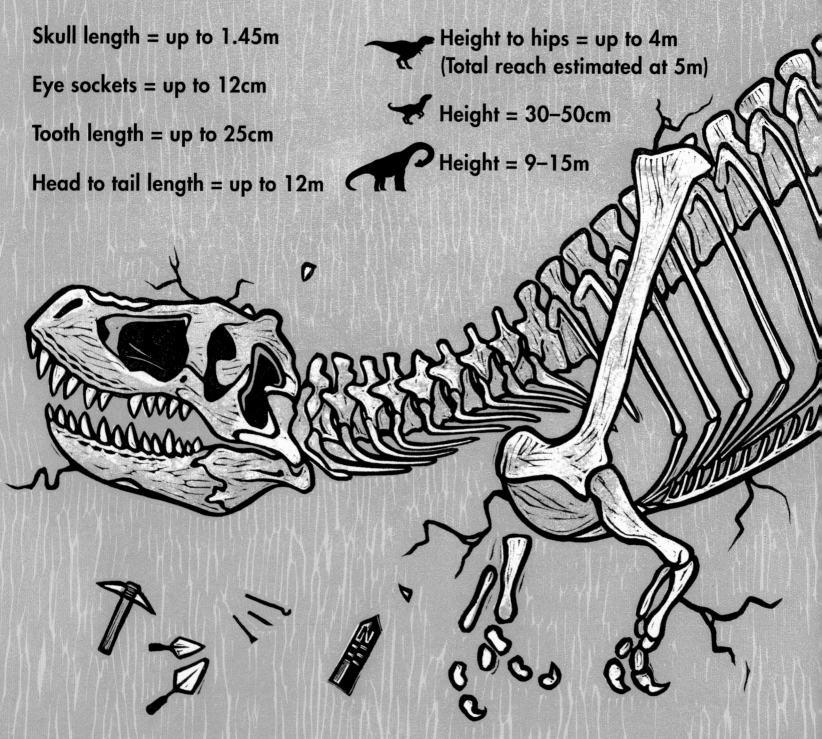

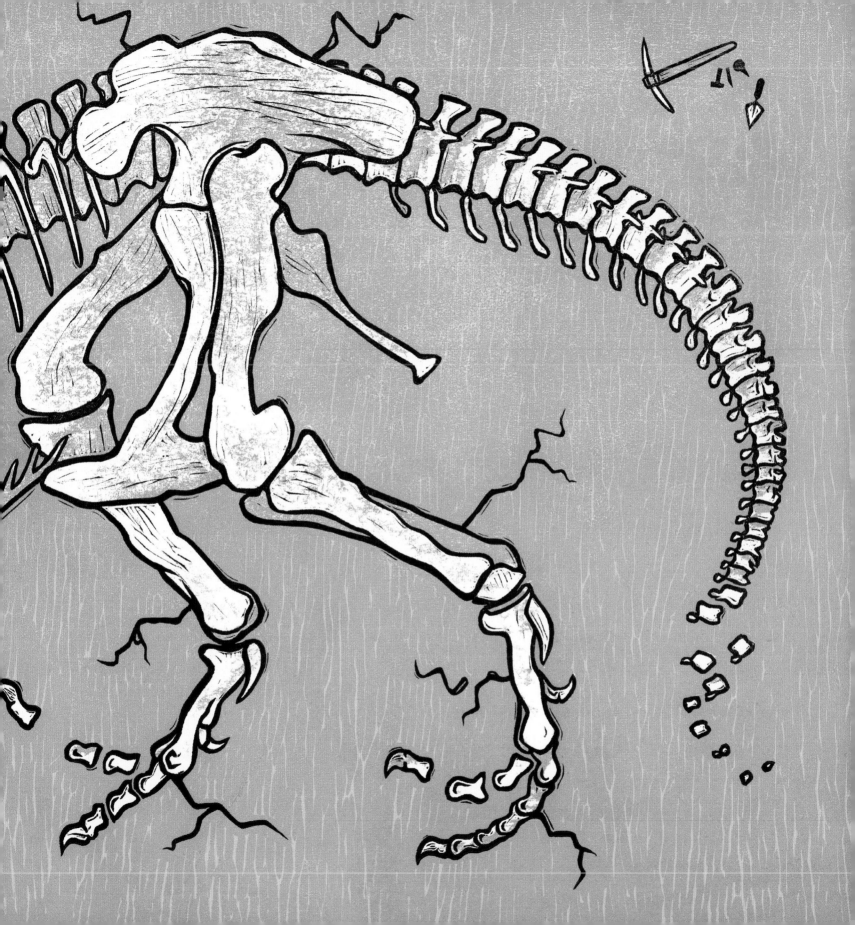

More Boxer Books to enjoy

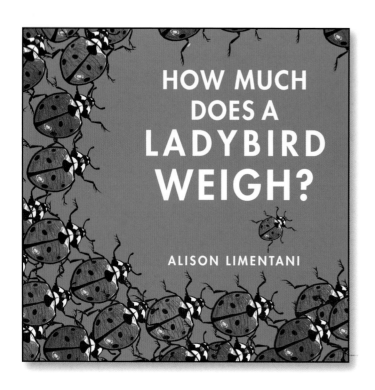

HOW MUCH DOES A LADYBIRD WEIGH?
by Alison Limentani

Have you ever wondered how much a ladybird weighs? What about the weight of a snail, a bird or even a swan? In Alison Limentani's extraordinary and original picture book she introduces us to a fascinating world of numbers, weight and wildlife.

HOW LONG IS A WHALE?
by Alison Limentani

Have you ever wondered how long a whale is? What about a shark, a dolphin or even a sea otter? In Alison Limentani's extraordinary and original picture book she introduces us to a fascinating world of numbers, length and wildlife.